MOVING / BEAUTIFULLY
BEAUTIFULLY / MOVING

This book is dedicated to

KIM WHITE

whose persistent optimism and generosity
has moved the Joffrey in innumerable ways.

Design: Chirp Design, Inc. / Print: Active Graphics, Inc.
Printed in Chicago, IL / USA

ISBN 978-0-692-94668-8

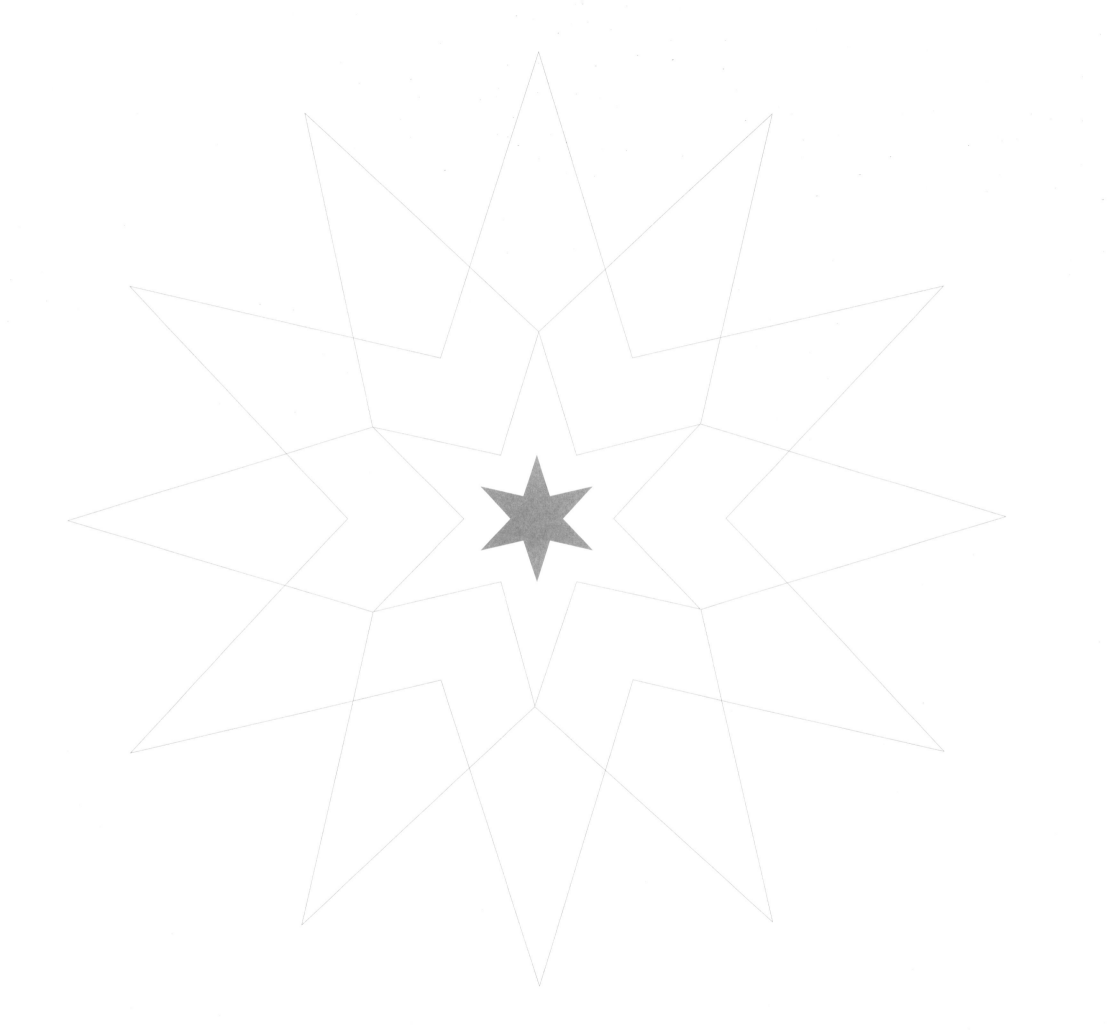

CONTENTS

WE SEE IN ORDER TO MOVE; WE MOVE IN ORDER TO SEE.

— WILLIAM GIBSON

In honoring the legacy of our founder — Robert Joffrey — I assure you that The Joffrey Ballet will never stop moving. Our commitment to the language of dance continues to grow and flourish under the visionary artistic leadership of Ashley Wheater — someone who has been "moving" from the early age of ten, when he enrolled in The Royal Ballet School.

I would argue that there is nothing "still" about the stunning photographs in this elegant volume that tell the story of Joffrey's history in its adopted home of Chicago. The Joffrey moved to Chicago during the tenure of Mayor Richard J. Daley and the incomparable first lady Maggie Daley. They both knew that Chicago would be a better city with a world-class ballet company as part of its cultural fabric. We thank them for their early support. Today, under the leadership of a dedicated Board of Directors, led by Honorary Chair Mayor Rahm Emanuel, dance in Chicago thrives. The Joffrey Ballet salutes our rich and diverse dance community — artists, choreographers, teaching artists, musicians, costume designers, photographers, and of course, the local, national, and international audiences that embrace William Gibson's reflection of movement. We indeed do "move in order to see."

I extend sincere thanks to all who have sustained us in the past and to those who continue to invest in our future.

Greg

Greg Cameron
Executive Director

The Joffrey Ballet owes its existence to Robert Joffrey: a brilliant teacher, choreographer, and director. He redefined ballet companies in the 20th century and brought an "American voice" to the art form. In the words of esteemed dance critic Anna Kisselgoff, "As The Joffrey Ballet looks to the future, it also remains reassuringly committed to its past. Distinct from other American ballet companies, it has sought to reflect the society in which we live."

The Joffrey Ballet continues to embrace its place and time.

In 1995, co-founder Gerald Arpino and a dedicated group of Joffrey friends moved the Company to Chicago. This "City of the Heartland" is a natural home for our very American dance company. We draw inspiration and strength from this dynamic place. Some of our most important work occurs amongst the people of the city, where we are enriched by their energy and diversity. Our Academy of Dance and Community Engagement programs introduce thousands of young people to the discipline, life skills, and joy found in dance.

New creations are the lifeblood of the Company. As Artistic Director of the Joffrey since 2007, I see my role as a curator and champion for an expanded repertoire. We seek excellence from a broad range of sources. We are proud to present new work by gifted choreographers while honoring our past by presenting classic stories in a new way. I hope you will find memories and inspiration within this volume.

Ashley Wheater
Artistic Director

BALLET IS A MOVEABLE FEAST FOR THE EYES, EARS, AND HEART, SPEAKING TO THE SOUL AND INTELLECT THROUGH THE ARTFUL MOVEMENT OF THE HUMAN BODY. THE JOFFREY BALLET EMBODIES THIS ART FORM, TAKING DANCE TO STUNNING HEIGHTS AND FAR-REACHING FOREFRONTS.

MOVING/ARTFULLY

CHAPTER 1 MOVING ARTFULLY

DANCE IS A WORDLESS MEANS OF COMMUNICATION

designed through movement to convey an emotion, express a thought, or tell a story. The Joffrey Ballet embraces this artistry with passion and precision. Joffrey dancers contribute body and soul to speak directly to the audience, capitalizing on their diversity, while still communicating as one graceful artistic ensemble.

TO PREPARE FOR PERFORMANCES, JOFFREY ARTISTS REHEARSE UP TO **1,000 HOURS** A SEASON.

PREPARATION involves a lifetime of dedication, mastering technique and deepening expression.

IN A BALLET LIKE *RAKU*,
I HAVE TO LET MYSELF BE
FULLY **IMMERSED** AND
PRESENT IN THE STORY, SO
THE **EMOTIONS** ARE REALLY
COMING FROM WITHIN.

— CHRISTINE ROCAS, JOFFREY ARTIST

THE SIMPLEST GESTURE, AND HOW
THAT GESTURE, THE MUSIC, AND THE MOVEMENT
GO TOGETHER, IS A VERY POWERFUL TOOL

— ASHLEY WHEATER, ARTISTIC DIRECTO

TO BE **VULNERABLE** ON STAGE, YOU HAVE TO DANCE WITH THE SAME **PASSION** IN THE STUDIO, AS IF IT WERE A **PERFORMANCE.**

— MIGUEL ANGEL BLANCO, JOFFREY ARTIST

DANCERS COME IN ALL **SHAPES** AND **SIZES**; TALENT DOESN'T COME IN ONE SHAPE.

— ROBERT JOFFREY, CO-FOUNDER OF THE JOFFREY BALLET

I LOOK FOR **INDIVIDUALITY**, NOT AN ABSOLUTE BODY TYPE. WE ALL POSSESS SOMETHING **UNIQUE**.

— ASHLEY WHEATER, ARTISTIC DIRECTOR

BEFORE THE DANCERS SET FOOT ON STAGE, a multitude of talented artists have collaborated to develop, enhance, and refine the work.

THE CHOREOGRAPHER
BEGINS WITH A **VISION**
WHERE THE STAGE IS A
BLANK CANVAS AND ADDS
MOVEMENT AND MUSIC.
MAKING THAT FIRST
BRUSHSTROKE IS LIKE
PAINTING MUSIC.

— CHRISTOPHER WHEELDON, CHOREOGRAPHER

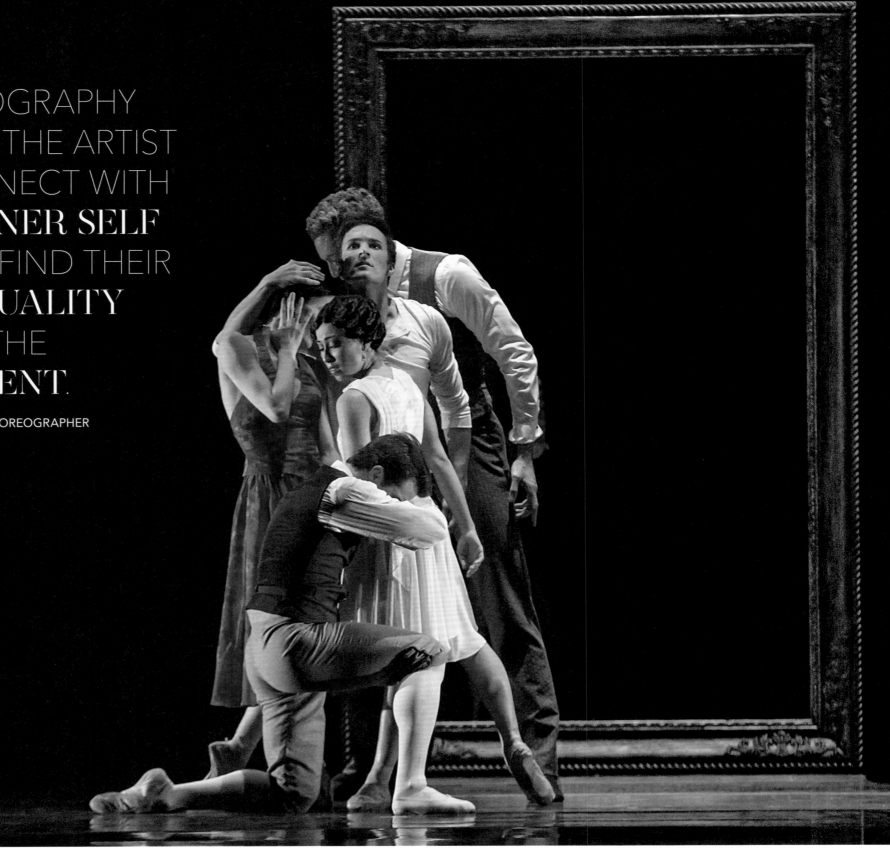

CHOREOGRAPHY ALLOWS THE ARTIST TO CONNECT WITH THEIR **INNER SELF** AND TO FIND THEIR **INDIVIDUALITY** WITHIN THE **MOVEMENT**.

— NICOLAS BLANC, CHOREOGRAPHER

VAL CANIPAROLI / ARIA

THE TECHNICAL PRECISION OF THE
JOFFREY DANCERS **BLENDS SEAMLESSLY** WITH
MY MORE ORGANIC CHOREOGRAPHY.

— BROCK CLAWSON, CHOREOGRAPHER

SEEING A NEW WORK COME ALIVE
IN FRONT OF US, TOGETHER,
IS THE BEST JOB IN THE WORLD.

— ALEXANDER EKMAN, CHOREOGRAPHER

BALLET IN THE JOFFREY'S HANDS IS ACCESSIBLE, PROVOCATIVE, FUN-LOVING, AND OFTEN SUBLIMELY BEAUTIFUL. —SID SMITH, *CHICAGO TRIBUNE*

ANNABELLE LOPEZ OCHOA / MAMMATUS

WHEN THE DANCERS ARE **STRUCK** BY THE **ARTISTRY** OF THE GODS, IMAGES OF FLOATING BIRDS IN **CLOUDS** CAN BE **ACHIEVED.** —ANNABELLE LOPEZ OCHOA, CHOREOGRAPHER

DANCE IS A **LANGUAGE** FOR THE EYES FOR THOSE WHO CAN SEE AND A **SENSATION** OF THE HEART FOR THOSE WHO CAN FEEL.

— LAR LUBOVITCH, CHOREOGRAPHER

WAYNE MCGREGOR / INFRA

THERE IS A
DANCER IN
EVERYBODY.

— WAYNE MCGREGOR, CHOREOGRAPHER

DANCE IS THE LIVING SHAPE OF EMOTION.

— JOHN NEUMEIER, CHOREOGRAPHER

MOVEMENT IS FOUND IN THE STUDIO WITH THE DANCERS.

— ASHLEY PAGE, CHOREOGRAPHER

KRZYSZTOF PASTOR / ROMEO & JULIET

JUSTIN PECK / IN CREASES

CHOREOGRAPHY, FOR ME, IS A **CELEBRATION** OF **MUSIC**. — JUSTIN PECK, CHOREOGRAPHER

THE JOFFREY BALLET IS SUCH AN ICONIC COMPANY
FULL OF UNIQUE, EXPLOSIVE, AND EXPRESSIVE ARTISTS.

WORKING WITH THEM HAS BEEN A TRUE HIGHLIGHT OF MY CAREER. —STANTON WELCH, CHOREOGRAPHER

COMPOSERS AND MUSICIANS BRING TO THE EARS WHAT THE DANCERS BRING TO THE EYES.

MY CHALLENGE AS CONDUCTOR IS TO COMMUNICATE THE SPECIFIC NEEDS OF THE STAGE, WITH MY BATON, TO MUSICIANS WHO CANNOT SEE THE DANCERS.

— SCOTT SPECK, JOFFREY MUSIC DIRECTOR

A BEAM OF **LIGHT**, A WASH OF **COLOR**, A FLOWING PIECE OF **FABRIC** – ARTISTIC ENHANCEMENTS ADD **DRAMA** AND **DEPTH**, CREATING A MAGICAL SPACE THAT TRANSCENDS THE EVERYDAY.

MOVING / MEANINGFULLY

CHAPTER

2

CHAPTER 2 MOVING MEANINGFULLY

THE JOFFREY BALLET'S REPERTOIRE EXPLORES

how movement, throughout time, has poignantly remarked upon human experience and revealed human emotion. Staking a claim in the international dance scene, the Joffrey engages in dance history by recreating past works, presenting current choreography, and promoting new pieces that move ballet forward. The range of its repertoire builds new lovers of ballet while keeping more traditional viewers curious and connected: celebrating the past, embracing the present, and driving the future.

HISTORIC REVIVALS

Reconstructing lost masterpieces and reworking historical landmarks upholds The Joffrey Ballet's important mission to learn from ballet's history as a foundation from which to launch ballet into the future.

I THINK THAT
BECAUSE WE
[AS AMERICANS]
DON'T HAVE
A BALLET
TRADITION,
WE CAN BREAK
TRADITION...
THAT IS ONE OF
OUR GREATEST
FREEDOMS.

— ROBERT JOFFREY,
    CO-FOUNDER OF THE JOFFREY BALLET

THROUGH THE **UNSPOKEN** WORD, THROUGH MOVEMENT, YOU CAN **ACCOMPLISH** SO MUCH.

— GERALD ARPINO, CO-FOUNDER OF THE JOFFREY BALLET

Robert Joffrey dreamed of including Ashton's iconic full-length story ballet in his Company's repertoire. In 2006, the Joffrey became the first American company to dance his *Cinderella*, which personifies the Ashton style.

DANCE IS MUSIC MADE **VISIBLE**.
DANCERS ARE INSTRUMENTS, LIKE A PIANO
THE CHOREOGRAPHER **PLAYS**. — GEORGE BALANCHINE

Recognized as a major work of German Expressionism, *The Green Table* was the first ballet Robert Joffrey ever saw. The impact of that experience prompted him to restage the ballet in 1967.

FORGOTTEN LAND IS THE PERFECT MELDING OF **MUSICALITY** AND **MOVEMENT;** GRITTY AND TENACIOUS WITH UNPARALLELED **DYNAMIC** ENERGY.

— ANASTACIA HOLDEN, JOFFREY ARTIST

WATERBABY BAGATELLES 1994 / NINE SINATRA SONGS 1982 / TWYLA THARP

Selecting which works to perform encapsulates the desire to entertain, to spark imaginations, to evoke feelings that are light or dark, joyous or melancholy, ponderous or gritty.

WHEN THE AUDIENCE **APPLAUDED** AT MY FIRST ENTRANCE, I IMMEDIATELY GOT **GOOSEBUMPS** AND **BUTTERFLIES** IN MY STOMACH. I THOUGHT, **THIS IS IT!** THIS IS WHAT I'VE TRAINED FOR.

— VICTORIA JAIANI, JOFFREY ARTIST

REIMAGINED CLASSICS

Bringing beloved ballets to the stage in a fresh and relevant way, reimagined classics provide audiences with stories that are familiar, yet cast anew.

LA BAYADÈRE / STANTON WELCH

WE **CHERISH** THE **CLASSICS** BECAUSE
THEY ARE THE **CENTER** OF OUR LANGUAGE.
BALLET IS OUR FOUNDATION, BUT IT IS
NOT THE **CIRCUMFERENCE** OF OUR WORLD.

— ASHLEY WHEATER, ARTISTIC DIRECTOR

OTHELLO / LAR LUBOVITCH

HARD WORK AND PERSEVERANCE IS THE DANCERS' MOTTO AND DISCIPLINE IS THEIR STRENGTH. OBSTACLES ONLY EXIST IF THEY SURRENDER TO THEM.

— FABRICE CALMELS, JOFFREY ARTIST

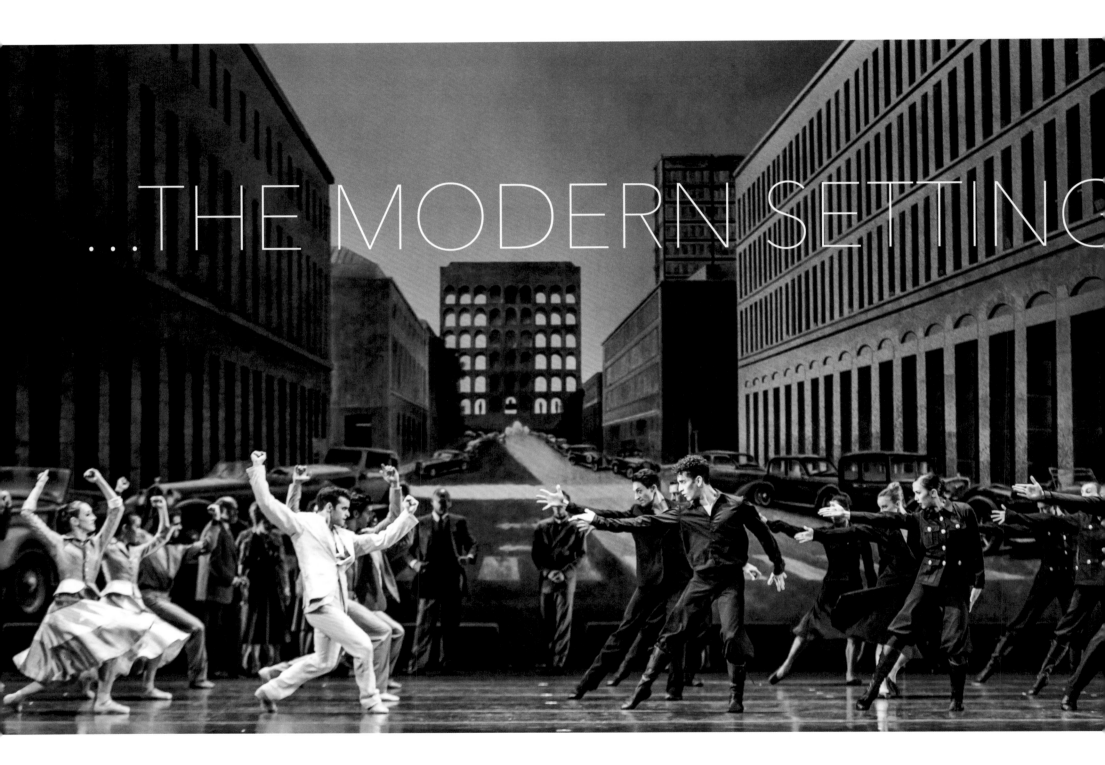

...THE MODERN SETTING

MAKES IT MATTER.

— LAURA MOLZAHN, *CHICAGO TRIBUNE*

TO BE ROMEO, TO **DISAPPEAR** INSIDE THE CHARACTER AND DANCE INSIDE HIS WORLD, WAS A **DREAM** COME TRUE.

— RORY HOHENSTEIN, JOFFREY ARTIST

SWAN LAKE / CHRISTOPHER WHEELDON

SYLVIA / JOHN NEUMEIER

THE JOFFREY'S **LEGACY** IS ONE OF GUTSY, INNOVATIVE PROGRAMMING.

— SID SMITH, *CHICAGO TRIBUNE*

CONTEMPORARY WORKS

Contemporary ballet,
in the hands of
The Joffrey Ballet,
expands boundaries and
redefines possibilities
for this poetic art form.

THE JOFFREY BALLET HAS LONG BEEN **KNOWN** FOR ITS VERSATILITY...

— JENNIFER DUNNING, *NEW YORK TIMES*

I THINK IT'S IMPORTANT TO TAKE **RISKS** TO FURTHER THE ART FORM AND MAKE SURE IT STILL FEELS **RELEVANT** AND **EXCITING.** — JUSTIN PECK, CHOREOGRAPHER

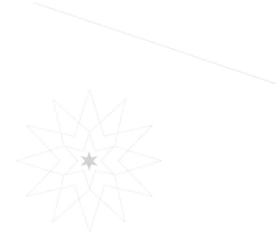

LITURGY / CHRISTOPHER WHEELDON

WHEELDON'S
WORKS ARE VERY
SATISFYING TO
PERFORM.
THEY ARE
CHALLENGING,
YET **FREEING**…
THEY FEEL GOOD
ON YOUR BODY.

— APRIL DALY, JOFFREY ARTIST

THE MAN IN BLACK / JAMES KUDELKA

RAKU / YURI POSSOKHOV

THE COMPANY
IS AWASH
IN **SUPERB**
DANCERS,
BUT THEY ARE
GIFTED ACTORS
AS WELL.

— HEDY WEISS, *CHICAGO SUN-TIMES*

TULLE / ALEXANDER EKMAN

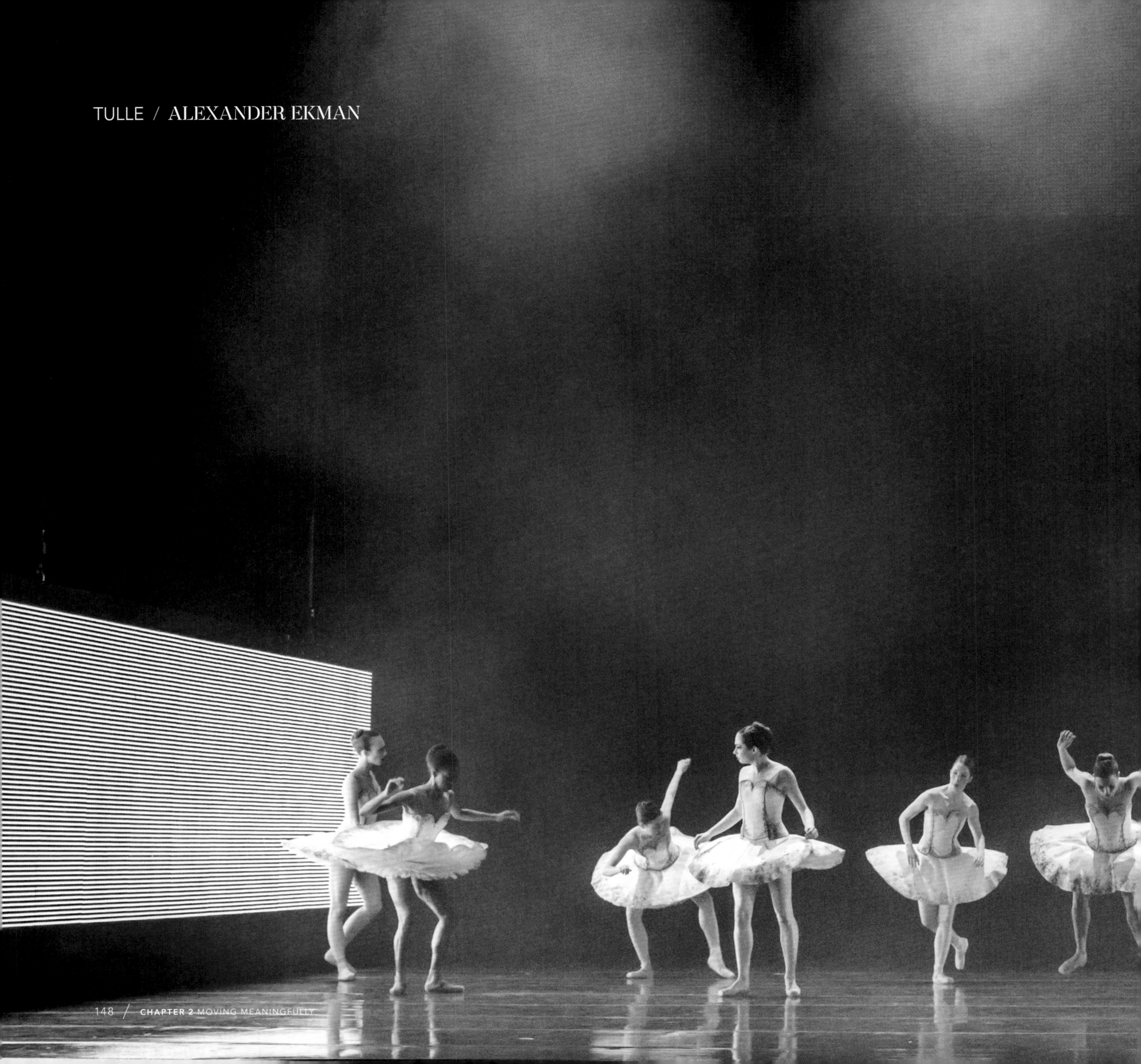

UNAFRAID TO PUSH THE BOUNDARIES OF BALLET EVEN FURTHER, THE JOFFREY BALLET BREAKS TRADITION TO MAKE MOVEMENT DISTINCTIVE, MEMORABLE, AND SOMETIMES UNCOMFORTABLE.

YEAR OF THE RABBIT / JUSTIN PECK

WORLD
PREMIERES

Participating in the most current and international dialogue by commissioning and producing works that challenge and advance, The Joffrey Ballet continues to be globally relevant.

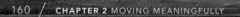

ADAGIO 2012 / YURI POSSOKHOV

THE **STRENGTH** AND **VERSATILITY** OF THE DANCERS MAKE THE JOFFREY **UNIQUE.**

— MYLES THATCHER, CHOREOGRAPHER

WHEN YOU
WATCH
THE JOFFREY
BALLET
WORK ITS
MAGIC, YOU
REALIZE THAT
DANCERS ARE
THE ULTIMATE
ATHLETES.

— LAURA MOLZAHN, *CHICAGO TRIBUNE*

THE VISUAL SIDE EXPLAINS A
LOT ABOUT THE MUSIC AND THE
MUSIC EXPLAINS A LOT ABOUT
WHAT YOU SEE, WHICH GIVES IT
EVEN MORE EMOTIONAL DEPTH.

— FRANZ WELSER-MÖST, CLEVELAND ORCHESTRA MUSIC DIRECTOR

HONEST HUMANITY AND **FIERCE** DANCING.

— LAUREN WARNECKE, *CHICAGO TRIBUNE*

I LOVE HOW **DIVERSE** THE COMPANY IS. THEY CAN SWITCH FROM **CLASSICAL** TO **CONTEMPORARY** IN A BLINK.

— ANNABELLE LOPEZ OCHOA, CHOREOGRAPHER

MOVING / CHICAGO

CHAPTER

3

JOFFREY AND CHICAGO

The Joffrey Ballet embraces its home in Chicago, sharing a strong work ethic and talent with this diverse international city. The Joffrey delivers a robust season, nurturing dance enthusiasts throughout the city and bringing ballet into areas of Chicago that would not otherwise be served by this art form.

Chicago's inspiring architectural backdrop is a match for beautiful
movement inside and outside the studio.

THE CITY IS OUR STAGE.

With the building of Joffrey Tower in 2008, the Company established even deeper roots in Chicago, underscoring its commitment to the arts and rich culture of the city.

Within its 45,000 square feet of space, Joffrey Tower enables the Company to train and rehearse, as well as houses the Joffrey Academy of Dance and Community Engagement classes and performances. The building also provides a home for a black box theater, box office, costume shop, and key administrative services.

4 full-time staff and up to 6 additional seasonal employees work in the Wardrobe Department

16 people run each show for wardrobe, hair and make-up

700 costumes go through the Costume shop during a season

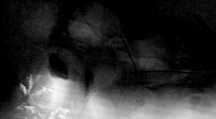

650
average pairs
of pointe shoes
used per season

$80
average cost of
pointe shoes

30
average pairs
of pointe shoes
used per ballerina
each season

ACADEMY

The Joffrey Academy of Dance, Official School of The Joffrey Ballet, invites hundreds of children and adults to find passion in dance, instructing them in artistic movements and inspiring them to discover their inner muse.

Barbara Levy Kipper & David A. Kipper Studio

The Joffrey Academy of Dance, under the leadership of Artistic Director Ashley Wheater, nurtures more than 2,500 students of all ages and backgrounds. Instilling deep loyalties and a long-term commitment to the Joffrey, the Academy succeeds in developing many students into Company dancers.

WINNING WORKS is a Joffrey program that awards diverse and emerging artists a platform for new choreography.

WINNING WORKS GIVES
OPPORTUNITIES TO
PEOPLE LIKE ME, WOMEN
CHOREOGRAPHERS,
AND PEOPLE OF COLOR.
IT IS SO IMPORTANT IN
PUSHING THE CRAFT
OF CONTEMPORARY
CHOREOGRAPHY TO NEW
AND EXCITING PLACES.

— STEPHANIE MARTINEZ,
    2015 WINNING CHOREOGRAPHER

Outside the Tower, the Joffrey broadens its reach into the community by bringing dance to many schools throughout the Chicago Public School system. In the Community Engagement programs, children learn about the art form while increasing personal discipline, self-confidence, physical strength, and fostering a deeper understanding and love of dance.

COMMUNITY ENGAGEMENT

The Joffrey Ballet is committed to bringing the joy of dance to as many people as possible.

I LIKE DANCING BECAUSE WHEN I DANCE, I FEEL SOMETHING LIKE A SPARKLE.

— CPS STUDENT

MOVING/FORWARD

CHAPTER 4

THE NUTCRACKER

When I first became Artistic Director of the Joffrey ten years ago, choreographer Christopher Wheeldon and I discussed creating a *Nutcracker*. From that spark, a fresh story and production have evolved. Set in Chicago during the time of the 1893 World's Columbian Exposition, elements of the original E.T.A. Hoffmann narrative dovetail nicely with a child's adventure at the exotic fairgrounds.

The World's Columbian Exposition placed a spotlight on Chicago, heralding its stature as a great American city. This was a time of optimism and dynamic growth. Imagine visiting the Fair, with its massive scale, gleaming architecture, exotic foreign pavilions, and raucous midway. For a visitor, young or old, the experience must have been marvelous. Chris and his creative team have captured this spirit in our new *Nutcracker*.

This *Nutcracker* tells the story of an immigrant mother and her two children, making their home in a new country. Many of us, including The Joffrey Ballet, arrived in Chicago from another place and found a home here. The creation of this new *Nutcracker* parallels the growth of the Joffrey and our embrace of the city.

— Ashley Wheater, Artistic Director

A GIFT OF ASTONISHMENTS... PURE MAGIC.

— HEDY WEISS, *CHICAGO SUN-TIMES*

EXTRAORDINARILY RICH, BEAUTIFUL AND EMOTIONALLY POTENT

— CHRIS JONES, *CHICAGO TRIBUNE*

APPENDIX

WE SHOULD CONSIDER EVERY **DAY** LOST ON WHICH WE HAVE NOT **DANCED** AT LEAST **ONCE**.

— FRIEDRICH NIETZSCHE

PHOTOGRAPHY

TABLE OF CONTENTS

CHAPTER 2 — MOVING MEANINGFULLY

(BEAUTY)

REPERTOIRE

2007–2017

ARTISTS
2007–2017

Heather Aagard 2001–2009	April Daly 2003–	Elizabeth Hansen 2006–2015	Suzanne Lopez 1991–2010	Valerie Robin 2000–2013	Alonso Tepetzi 2016–
Matthew Adamczyk 2005–	Fernando Duarte 2013–	Jaime Hickey 2009–2013	Greig Matthew 2017–	Christine Rocas 2005–	Kathleen Thielhelm 2000–2009
Derrick Agnoletti 2005–	Jonathan Dummar 2005–2011	William Hilliard 2006–2009	Graham Maverick 2008–	Paulo Rodrigues 2015–2017	Jack Thorpe–Baker 2010–2013
Yoshihisa Arai 2012–	Olivia Duryea 2017–	Rory Hohenstein 2011–	Erin McAfee 2008–2011	Aaron Rogers 2006–2014	Elivelton Tomazi 2013–
Amanda Assucena 2013–	Erica Lynette Edwards 2001–2015	Anastacia Holden 2005–2017	Brian McSween 1998–2009	Ricardo Santos 2010–2013	Shane Urton 2010–2014
Artur Babajanyan 2014–2017	Camila Ferrera 2015–2016	Dara Holmes 2011–	Caitlin Meighan 2008–2015	Tanner Schwartz 2009–2010	Alberto Velazquez 2011–
Edson Barbosa 2014–	Yumelia Garcia 2009–2014	Riley Horton 2016–	Jeraldine Mendoza 2011–	Lucas Segovia 2010–2016	Mauro Villanueva 2002–2013
Guillaume Basso 2012–2015	Cara Marie Gary 2012–	Yuka Iwai 2017–	Mona Meng 2010–2011	Chloé Sherman 2016–	Allison Walsh 2005–2011
Miguel Angel Blanco 2009–	Brian Gephart 2008–2011	Victoria Jaiani 2003–	Katherine Minor 2011–2013	Willy Shives 1999–2008	Jennifer Wang 2014–2015
Oğulcan Borova 2011–2015	Anna Gerberich 2015–2016	Hansol Jeong 2015–	Jacqueline Moscicke 2010–	Tian Shuai 2005–2011	Mahallia Ward 2011–2017
Katherine Bruno 2011–2013	John Mark Giragosian 2008–2015	Gayeon Jung 2015–	Amber Neumann 2009–2015	Abigail Simon 2006–2013	Jennifer Warnick 2007–2009
Anais Bueno 2013–	John Gluckman 2002–2009	Yumi Kanazawa 2016–	Thomas Nicholas 2003–2009	Patrick Simoniello 1994–2002 2006–2010	Maia Wilkins 1991–2008
Fabrice Calmels 2001–	David Gombert 2002–2010	Stacy Joy Keller 1999–2011	Emily Patterson 1999–2009	Michael Smith 2001–2013	Jenny Winton 2009–2014
Raúl Casasola 2008–	Stefan Goncalvez 2015–	Calvin Kitten 1992–2010	Eduardo Permuy 2006–2008	Aaron Smyth 2013–2015	Joanna Wozniak 2003–
Valeriia Chaykina 2015–	Luis Eduardo Gonzalez 2015–	Michael Levine 1993–1995 1997–2008	Alexis Polito 2006–2015	Lauren Stewart 2006–2009	Joan Sebastián Zamora 2015–
Nicole Ciapponi 2015–	Jennifer Goodman 1993–2009	Brooke Linford 2014–	Megan Quiroz 2004–2010	Temur Suluashvili 2003–	Kara Zimmerman 2009–2015
Lucia Connolly 2016–	Dylan Gutierrez 2009–	Fabio Lo Giudice 2011–2013	Aaron Renteria 2016–	Olivia Tang-Mifsud 2016–	

The Joffrey Family is incredible — from our subscribers to our dedicated Board of Directors, the generous corporate sponsors and loyal ticket buyers, our enthusiastic Women's Board and Joffrey Auxiliary Board members, and the many foundations and individuals who have sustained the Joffrey over its history. Dance is meant to be shared — and it is because of you, our loyal supporters, that the Joffrey is able to share its unique American Style with the world.

I extend my profound thanks for being a part of the Joffrey's past, present, and bright future.

Zachary D. Lazary, Jr.
Chair, Joffrey Board of Directors

LIGHTS OUT. CURTAIN DOWN.

DANCE IS MOVEMENT MADE BEAUTIFUL.

THE JOFFREY BALLET CONTINUES TO

ADVANCE DANCE AS AN ART FORM —

FOREVER IN MOTION,

MOVING BEAUTIFULLY

AND

BEAUTIFULLY MOVING.

MOVING BEAUTIFULLY/
BEAUTIFULLY MOVING CELEBRATES
ASHLEY WHEATER AND HIS YEARS
OF ARTISTIC LEADERSHIP AT THE
JOFFREY BALLET.

BRAVO
**TO ASHLEY AND THE GENEROUS INDIVIDUALS
WHO MADE THIS VOLUME POSSIBLE:**

Kim and Miles White

Sandy and Roger Deromedi
Patti S. Eylar and Charlie R. Gardner
Shelley and Bill Farley
Katherine and Richard Freiburger
Mr. and Mrs. John W. Higgins
Mr. and Mrs. David H. Hoffmann
Karen Gray-Krehbiel and John Krehbiel
Maggie and Eric Scheyer
Amelia and Alejandro Silva
Mr. and Mrs. Edward B. Smith, Jr.
Maria Smithburg and Bill Smithburg
Pamela and Russ Strobel
Hilary and Barry Weinstein

THE JOFFREY BALLET THANKS our performing artists, photographer Cheryl Mann and the many other photographers who captured their work, for allowing their images to be included in this book. Additional thanks to the students participating in Joffrey programs, our instructors, and dedicated Boards led by Zachary D. Lazar, Jr., and Patti S. Eylar. Thanks to Executive Director Greg Cameron for his tireless advocacy and passion for the arts. Thanks to Lynda Van Duerm of Chirp Design, Inc. and Project Manager Vicki Crain. Special thanks to Kim White and Maggie Scheyer for their dedication, passion, keen eye for detail, and editorial contributions. This volume is a testament to the talents of many and for the enjoyment of all.